First published 2013 by Kingfisher
This edition published 2016 by Kingfisher
an imprint of Macmillan Children's Books
20 New Wharf Road, London N1 9RR
Associated companies throughout the world
www.panmacmillan.com

Illustrations by: Peter Bull Art Studio

ISBN 978-0-7534-4115-2

1 3 5 7 9 8 6 4 2
1TR/0516/UTD/WKT/128MA

A CIP catalogue record for this book is available from
the British Library.

Printed in China

Picture credits

The Publisher would like to thank the following
for permission to reproduce their material.
(t = top, b = bottom, c = centre, l = left, r = right):
Pages 4 Naturepl/Tony Heald; 5tl Shutterstock/Eric Isselee;
5tr Shutterstock/palko72; 5cl Corbis/Tom Brakefield; 5cr Corbis/
Roger Wood; 5bc Samantha Richiardi; 6 Shutterstock/Nagel
Photography; 8c Photolibrary/Oxford Scientific Films (OSF);
8bl Shutterstock/Heather McCann; 9tl Getty/Karine Aigner/
National Geographic; 9tr Alamy/Purestock; 9cr Photoshot/NHPA;
9bl Shutterstock/pixelparticle; 10 Shutterstock/Mirek Srb;
12cl Photoshot/NHPA; 12cr Shutterstock/Dennis W Donohue;
13tl Alamy/Juniors Bildarchiv GmbH; 13tr Corbis/Daniel J. Cox;
13cr Photolibrary/OSF; 13bl Getty/Martin Harvey/Gallo Images;
13br Corbis/Daniel J. Cox; 14 Shutterstock/EcoPrint; 16tl Naturepl/
Richard du Toit; 16cr Frank Lane Picture Agency (FLPA)/Winfried
Wisniewski; 16cl Photoshot/NHPA; 17tl Naturepl/Susi Eszterhas;
17tr Ardea/Thomas Marent; 17bl Shutterstock/Daleen Loest;
17br FLPA/Jurgen & Christine Sohns; 18 Shutterstock/photobar;
20bl Alamy/Mike Hill; 21tl Superstock/James Urbach; 21tr FLPA/
Pete Oxford/Minden; 21c Naturepl/Carine Schrurs; 21bl Naturepl/
Anup Shah; 21br FLPA/David Hosking; 22 FLPA/Richard du Toit/
Minden; 24cl FLPA/Michael Krebs/Imagebroker; 24cr Getty/Anup
Shah/The Image Bank; 24bl FLPA/Suzi Eszterhas/Minden;
24br Getty/Panoramic Images; 25t FLPA/Photo Researchers;
25b FLPA/Richard du Toit/Minden; 26 FLPA/Michael Durham/
Minden; 28cr Corbis/Zhang Xiaoli/Xinhua Press; 28b FLPA/Fritz
Polking; 29l Naturepl/Luiz Claudio Marigo; 29tc Corbis/Alexandra
Boulat; 29tr Naturepl/Andy Rouse; 29br Alamy/Purestock;
30tr FLPA/Elliot Neep; 30ctl Shutterstock/Stephen Meese;
30cbl Shutterstock/Andy Poole; 30cbr FLPA/Terry Whitaker;
30bl Superstock/Juniors; 30br Shutterstock/Stuart G Porter;
31tr Shutterstock/Cheryl Ann Quigley; 31ctl Shutterstock/Galyna
Andrushko; 31ctr Alamy/Arco Images; 31bl Photolibrary/Peter
Arnold Images; 31br Shutterstock/EcoPrint.

Contents

More to explore

On some of the pages in this book, you will find coloured buttons with symbols on them. There are four different colours, and each belongs to a different topic. Choose a topic, follow its coloured buttons through the book, and you'll make some interesting discoveries of your own.

For example, on page 6 you'll find a green button, like this, next to a wetland scene. The green buttons are about places around the world where big cats live.

Page 27

World

There is a page number in the button. Turn to that page (page 27) to find a green button on another place where big cats live. Follow all the steps through the book, and at the end of your journey you'll find out how the steps are linked, and discover even more information about this topic.

Cat cousins

Record breakers

Prey animals

The other topics in this book are cat cousins, record breakers and prey animals. Follow the steps and see what you can discover!

What are big cats?

Lions, tigers, leopards and jaguars are all big cats. These animals are powerful hunters with sharp claws and teeth. Some big cats live in tropical areas but others are found in cooler places. Many have been hunted for their fur and are now endangered.

Adult male lions have a shaggy mane.

The African lion is one of the world's top hunters. Big cats are carnivores – they eat only meat, and first they have to catch it. They are strong and stealthy and have plenty of weapons to kill their prey.

plenty of muscle

sharp teeth and strong jaws

long, fast legs

a hungry lion on the prowl

powerful paws

sharp claws

Big cats have beautiful fur coats.

a jaguar's coat

A long-legged serval rests on the grass.

a tigress with her three cubs

The serval is one of about 35 smaller wild cats. Others include the ocelot and the lynx. Wild cats are related to big cats but, unlike their larger cousins, they cannot roar.

The ancient Egyptians made beautiful statues of cats.

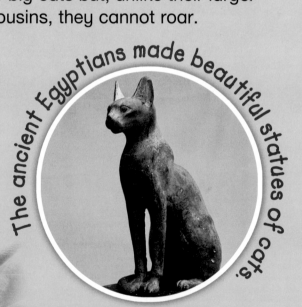

A female tiger feeds and protects her young until they can look after themselves. Big cats are mammals. Baby cubs grow inside their mother's body for about 3 months. Then she gives birth to them and feeds them on her milk.

Pet cats belong to the same family as wild cats. Cats first lived with people 5,000 years ago. They guarded stores of food from mice. Now cats are our companions.

The perfect cat

Every part of a cat's body helps it to move, hunt and survive. Strong muscles make it fast and agile. Sharp senses – sight, hearing and smell – alert it to food or danger. The cat's size and power and its jaws and claws help it to catch prey.

③

②

①

What is this?

Page 27

① A pair of green iguanas climb up a tree.

② A black howler monkey calls the alarm.

③ A hyacinth macaw flies off, squawking.

? This is a peccary's snout. Peccaries look like wild pigs and are prey for jaguars.

Page 22

In the wetlands of Brazil, a jaguar pounces on a caiman lurking in the water. The caiman has little chance of escape. Jaguars are at home in water. They are strong swimmers with muscular bodies and a powerful bite. Nearby animals call out warnings and hurry away.

Page 15

4 A startled stork makes its escape.

5 Wetlands are made up of marshes and pools.

6 Caimans are alligators that live in fresh water.

Amazing bodies

Big cats are some of the world's most agile animals. Powerful and beautiful, they can run, leap, pounce, stalk, climb and swim. From their sharp eyes and ears to their long, strong tail, every part of their body has adapted for survival in the wild.

Long, bendy spine can flex and stretch.

Long tail helps the body to balance.

Strong muscles power the lightweight frame.

A **cheetah** has a long, supple spine (backbone) that allows it to stretch its long legs to the limit. In a life-or-death chase after its prey, the cheetah can cover 7 metres in a single bound.

soft pads under the paws help with silent stalking.

a lion cub's paw

The lynx works out the world around it using superb senses. Forward-facing eyes judge distances well. Long ears turn to pick up every rustle. Stiff, sensitive whiskers help the cat to judge gaps and spaces, and to feel its way.

Sharp, curved claws grip prey and help with climbing.

The margay spends most of its life in the trees. It is an acrobatic climber. Its broad feet, flexible toes and strong claws help to give it a good grip. Its long tail helps it to balance.

A margay climbs down head first.

A leopard stays fully alert as it drinks at a waterhole at night. Its eyes have a shiny backing, which boosts the light of the moon and stars, helping the cat to see in the dark.

Eyes catch the light and seem to glow.

Page 22

What is this?

1 Snow leopards may hunt in pairs.

2 Smoky grey fur blends in with the rocky, snowy ground.

3 Large paws work like snowshoes.

Habitat for a cat

The place where an animal lives is called its habitat. Big cats live in many different habitats. Some live in tropical forests. Others need grassy plains or rocky mountains. Wherever an animal lives, its habitat provides it with food and shelter, and space to hunt and roam.

Page 30

6

4

5

In the harsh mountains of Central Asia, two young snow leopards are hunting. Teaming up gives them a greater chance of success. Strong and sure-footed, they leap over a ravine to chase game birds in the snow. Their long tails help them to balance. Higher up, wild sheep graze on scrubby grass. They, too, are a snow leopard's prey.

This is a snow leopard's nose. The large nostrils help to suck in more of the thin, mountain air.

All sorts of homes

Deserts, forests, mountains, marshes – big cats are found in a wide range of places. Most species live in a particular habitat. Over thousands of years, they have developed skills and features that help them to survive in their home landscape and climate.

Caracals live in dry scrub. They get by on little water.

A sandy coat blends in with the background.

The Siberian tiger is found in the **mountain forests** of southeast Russia. It lives further north than any other kind of tiger. Its large size and thick fur help it to survive winter temperatures of –45°C.

at home in
the desert

The **cougar**, also known as the puma and the mountain lion, has adapted to many different habitats. It is found in forests, deserts, wetlands and mountains in North and South America.

Panthers are expert climbers, at home in the trees. This one is a black leopard in a **tropical forest** in Africa. Black-coated jaguars in the Amazon rainforest are also called panthers.

Cougars have even been seen in towns.

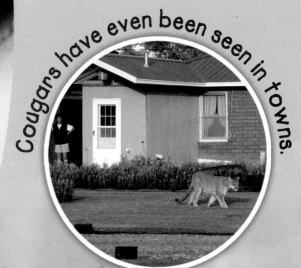

a serval
stalking
water rats

at home in the
mountains

Servals hunt in **marshes and lakes**. Their long ears help them to hunt, pinpointing the rustles of rats, birds and frogs hidden in the reeds.

Page 30

1 African wild dogs may try to steal the kill.

2 The approaching lions stay low.

3 Each lion is just a short sprint away from its prey.

What is this?

Hunting together

A pride of lions lives together and hunts together, too. A group of them will stalk and attack their prey, and then share the kill with the others. Teamwork helps lions to hunt animals much bigger than themselves. Other big cats cannot do this because they hunt alone.

4 Two young males join in the hunt.

5 Cape buffalo are bulky and fierce, and often see off lions.

6 Most hunting starts at dusk, as the light fades.

15

5

6

Page 26

Page 11

On the grasslands of Africa, a group of lionesses are stalking buffalo. The cats grunt softly to each other, inching forwards into the breeze so that their scent will not carry to their prey. They crouch low to stay hidden. One of them spots a weaker animal and suddenly sprints towards it. The others move in to help with the kill.

This is a buffalo's long, curving horn. The sharp horns are dangerous and can injure lions.

Cheetahs hunt fast-running antelope. When the cat gets near enough, it reaches out a paw to trip its prey. As the antelope loses balance, the hunter grabs it by the throat.

A caracal can pluck birds out of the air. It pushes down on its back legs, leaps off the ground and bats at prey with its paws.

Large paws strike birds in mid-air.

Lions sometimes lose their hard-won meals to scavengers such as hyenas. Spotted hyenas are fierce and aggressive and, if their pack outnumbers the lions, will rob them of their kill.

Killer cats

Big cats are fearsome hunters. Most of them stalk, chase and then pounce on their prey, clamping their jaws around its throat until it chokes and dies. A successful kill must be gobbled up fast or it may be stolen by scavengers – meat-eaters, such as hyenas or vultures, that feed on animal remains.

A lioness and her cub suck and crunch zebra bones.

a mess of juicy meat and bone

Back teeth crack bones and slice meat.

Long, sharp fangs stab and tear.

Small front teeth nibble flesh from the bone.

A leopard quickly protects its kill before other animals can smell it. The cat drags the carcass into a tree where scavengers cannot follow.

A leopard carries its kill in its mouth.

The jaguar has the most powerful bite of any cat. Unlike other big cats, it kills its prey not by suffocation but by biting clean through the skull. It then uses its teeth to open the carcass and tear meat from the bones.

Cats have a rough tongue to lick bones clean.

Cat quarrels

Big cats live in different ways. Most species live alone but young male cheetahs stay together, often for the whole of their lives. They find a hunting ground with food, water and females for breeding. They guard this territory from other cheetahs and will fight to the death to defend it.

What are these?

Page 14

 Two male cheetahs stand their ground.

 Cats flatten their ears when angry or afraid.

③ Gemsbok antelope graze on the scrub.

? These are a cheetah's bared teeth. The row of sharp, white teeth makes the cat look more threatening.

On their hunting ground in the Kalahari desert in Africa, two cheetahs meet an intruder. It is another male, hungry and hunting for food. The angry cats glare at it, crouching low and growling. The stranger understands the signs and the choice before it. It can fight and maybe get hurt – or turn around and leave.

3

Page 30

4

5

6

A solo male is looking for territory.

5
Cats crouch low when they are ready to attack.

Grasses and thorny shrubs grow in the red sand.

Getting along

Most big cats live alone. Individuals from the same species spread out to avoid competing for prey. They communicate with each other across large distances, using sound, scent and visual signs to get their message across.

Most lions roar at dawn and dusk.

An adult male lion roars loudly to keep other lions off its patch. Big cats tend to keep out of each other's way. It helps them to avoid fights and life-threatening injuries.

When a **female jaguar** is ready to mate, she broadcasts the news around the forest with loud calls and special scent markings. These help males within her range to track her down.

male jaguar

female jaguar

a snow leopard hunting for a meal

Lions are the only big cats to live in groups. Most prides are made up of about 15 animals – one or two males, five or six females and a handful of youngsters and cubs.

A snow leopard spends most of its life alone, except during the breeding season. Prey can be scarce in the mountains so adults need a large territory to help them to survive.

A caracal scratches a tree with its claws. The marks are a sign for others to see. They say, 'Trespassers, keep out! This territory is taken!'.

A female tiger signals to males by spraying her scent on a tree.

What is this?

① These cubs are 6 to 7 weeks old.

② Play-fighting helps the cubs to grow stronger.

③ Eagles could attack young cubs.

Page 15

Page 18

Mother and cubs

Before a female cat gives birth she has to find a den, such as an old burrow or a thick bush. Here, her cubs are hidden from danger and sheltered from the weather. The mother feeds and raises the cubs on her own. She has to leave them behind in the den when she goes out hunting.

Page 11

Four leopard cubs relax outside the den where they were born. Their mother is washing one of them. Two more are play-fighting with each other, practising skills they will soon need for hunting. The female leopard stays alert. She will move the cubs back inside the den if she senses danger.

4

5

6

This is the mother leopard's tongue. Its rough texture helps to clean the cubs' fur.

Family life

Raising a litter is hard work. From the moment her tiny cubs are born, a mother cat feeds and protects them. They may be with her for more than two years. She will teach them everything she knows about hunting and survival.

A lynx mother cleans her newborn cub.

...... *Newborn cubs are blind and helpless.*

A lioness carries a cub in her mouth while two more follow alongside. Big cats use their teeth very gently to grasp the loose skin at the back of their cub's neck.

A cheetah feeds her 9-day-old cubs. For the first weeks, cubs feed only on milk. The mother must eat meat so that her body can produce nourishing milk. She leaves her babies while she hunts.

A cheetah cub eats meat caught by its mother.

...... *The cub is 8 weeks old.*

Young cubs learn as they play. Bigger cubs often 'hunt' one another – learning to climb, balance, stalk and pounce. They do not bite for real and they keep their sharp claws in – most of the time!

Tiger cubs spend a lot of time playing.

The cub in front makes a clumsy attempt to pounce.

Cheetah cubs begin to learn to hunt from the age of about 12 weeks. Their mother brings home live prey so that they can practise how to kill.

Saving big cats

Tigers and other big cats face a difficult future. In our crowded world there is less space for them to hunt and breed. Hungry tigers attack farm animals and, sometimes, humans too. Just a few thousand tigers live in the wild. If we do not help them fast, they could become extinct.

Page 30

What is this?

1 Walkie-talkies help forest workers to keep in touch.

2 The tiger has been drugged.

3 The collar tracks the tiger using satellite technology.

? This is a tiger's footprint. Each tiger has its own unique prints, which can be used to identify it.

Page 23

In a rainforest in India, a Bengal tiger sleeps on the ground. Conservation workers have tranquillized the animal so that they can put on a special collar. One worker is fixing a camera to a tree. The collar and camera will track the tiger's movements – helping to keep it away from humans and out of harm's way.

(4) The workers use a jeep to travel through the forest.

(5) This gun was used to fire the tranquillizer dart.

(6) Camera traps provide information about tigers.

People and big cats

Humans harm big cats. We destroy their habitat, hunt their prey and some people even kill them for their skins. Yet humans also help big cats. Scientists study them, while others set up reserves where cats can live safely.

A female leopard watches **farmers'** cows. Big cats often go hungry as people take over their habitats and hunt their prey. Yet if they attack people's livestock, the cats will probably be shot.

Big cats are still used in circuses in some parts of the world.

A leopard watches Masai herders and their cattle in Kenya.

Cats lose their habitat when forests are destroyed.

Tourists pay to see big cats in the wild. The money pays for conservation work. It also helps to support locals and discourage them from hunting.

People build homes or farms on the cleared land.

Zoos study and breed big cats. They also inspire and educate visitors, and help to raise funds for conservation work overseas.

The fur trade is a serious threat to big cats. Each year, thousands of animals are hunted for their fur, even though this is illegal. This official has seized jaguar skins from a criminal gang.

Record breakers

The snow leopard is a **long-jump champion**. It has been known to cross ravines 14m wide – ten times the length of its own body!

snow leopard

Weighing less than 60kg, leopards are the smallest big cats. Yet they are the **strongest climbers**. An adult male can drag a carcass three times its own weight up a tree.

World

Jaguars live in Central and South America, mostly in the Amazon rainforest. There are only about 15,000 of them left in the wild.

Tigers live in Asia, in areas dotted from China to the far east of Russia. There are about 3,500 tigers left in the wild.

Cat cousins

The wetlands of Brazil are home to **ocelots** as well as jaguars. They are smaller than jaguars and hunt smaller prey, such as fish, crabs, turtles and lizards. Like jaguars, they are hunted for their beautiful fur.

Leopards sometimes hunt the **African golden cat**. This cat lives in thick scrubland and forests, and hunts at night.

Prey animals

The Yacaré caiman looks like a small alligator. It lives in fresh water in the wetlands and rainforests of South America. It feeds on snails, snakes, piranhas and other fish.

caiman

Cape buffalo live in herds of more than 1,000 animals. They graze on grass at night, and rest during the day. If a buffalo is attacked, the other animals in the herd rush to its defence.

More to explore

Cheetahs are the **fastest animals** on land, reaching a top speed of 110km/h in less than 4 seconds. Large nostrils and lungs supply them with all the oxygen they need during these sudden bursts of energy.

paws like running shoes

Lions, tigers, leopards and jaguars are the only cats that can roar. Of these, the lion is the **loudest** with a roar that can be heard more than 8km away.

a leopard in scrubby grassland, Africa

Leopards cover the largest range of any wild cat – from central and east Africa to India, southeast Asia and China. They are doing well in Africa, but elsewhere their numbers are falling.

Snow leopards live in the mountains of central Asia. Their range covers an area the size of Greenland but this is spread over 12 countries. There are fewer than 7,000 snow leopards left in the wild.

Africa's grasslands are famous for lions, but medium-sized cats called **caracals** live there too. They have sharp hearing, and are so fast that they can catch antelope and hares.

large ears

In the same forests as tigers, **clouded leopards** live and hunt. These medium-sized cats are excellent climbers. They prey on monkeys, porcupines and deer.

chukor partridge

Chukor partridges live in small flocks on rocky hillsides throughout Asia. The birds feed on seeds, roots and ants. In winter, they move to the shelter of the lower slopes.

A gemsbok is a kind of antelope with spear-like horns. It feeds on herbs, grasses, shrubs and roots. It is well adapted to desert life and can survive for weeks without water.

Index